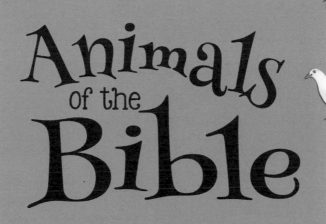

Animals
of the
Bible

christian art kids

© 2017 Christian Art Kids,
an imprint of Christian Art Publishers,
PO Box 1599, Vereeniging, 1930, RSA

359 Longview Drive, Bloomingdale, IL, 60108, USA

First edition 2017

Cover designed by Christian Art Kids

Illustrations by Catherine Groenewald

Unless otherwise indicated, all Scripture quotations are taken from the *Holy Bible*,
New Living Translation®, copyright © 1996, 2004, 2007, 2013, 2015
by Tyndale House Foundation. Used by permission of Tyndale House Publishers, Inc.,
Carol Stream, Illinois 60188. All rights reserved.

Scripture quotations marked CEV are taken from the *Holy Bible*,
Contemporary English Version®. Copyright © 1995 by American Bible Society.
All rights reserved.

Scripture quotations marked NCV are taken from the *Holy Bible*,
New Century Version®. Copyright © 2005 by Thomas Nelson.
Used by permission. All rights reserved.

Printed in China

ISBN 978-1-4321-1699-6

17 18 19 20 21 22 23 24 25 26 – 10 9 8 7 6 5 4 3 2 1

Foreword

I grew up in a family that adored animals. But the person who made me realize that animals are more than just our friends is my granddad Jan.

I remember how we used to sit outside during the early evenings. He taught me to listen to the neighborhood dogs as they barked at each other before settling down for the night. He also taught me never to kill anything – not even the tiniest ant – because I could never bring that body back to life again. Only God can. He showed me how wonderful it is to release a turtledove. For a moment the fluttering in your hands is astonishing. Then suddenly your hands are empty and your little friend is just a speck in the distance.

Although I was a city girl, Granddad's pile of *Farmer's Weekly* magazines and the stories about his childhood on the farm ensured that we had a small petting zoo of our own in the backyard. Only my dream of a cow wearing a jersey, and a female goose wearing a small hood and an apron (I was a Beatrix Potter fan) were never realized.

Today, nearly four decades later, I look in the green eyes of my cat Pieternella and realize that we both know that God loves us more than we could possibly understand. And the greatest thing of all is we can understand each other without speaking one word, because God's voice is in our hearts. While I was working on these animal stories, Pieternella spent all day on the blue armchair next to my desk. We trust that each of these animal stories from the Bible will remind you of the wonderful world God has created and how much He truly loves you.

Let's show God how much we love Him by protecting our animal friends.

Wendy Maartens & Pieternella

Contents

Noah's Animal Friends

Noah did everything the LORD had told him to do. His wife, his sons, and his daughters-in-law all went inside with him. He obeyed God and took a male and a female of each kind of animal and bird into the boat with him.

Genesis 7:7-9 CEV

I love my puppy very much. Every afternoon when I get home from school, she wags her little tail with joy. It is her way of saying, "Please don't leave again."

My cat purrs and brushes against my leg. That is her way of saying, "I'm so glad you're home."

My parrot calls, "Polly wants a cracker!" That is his way of saying, "Play with me too!" Mom comes in from the kitchen. "You have so many pets, it feels like we live in the ark," she laughs.

The Bible tells us about someone who really did live with a whole bunch of animals in an ark. His name was Noah. God loved Noah and his family. He wanted to save their lives. So God asked Noah to build a big boat called an ark. It was very hard work. The bad people made fun of Noah and his family for building the ark.

When the ark was ready, two of each animal on earth went into the ark. Finally, Noah and his family went into the ark. God Himself locked the door behind them.

It rained for 40 days and 40 nights. There was not a single mountaintop in sight. All the bad people outside of the ark drowned in the flood. Only Noah, his family and his animal friends survived.

God kept them safe, just like He promised!

Us and Our Animal Friends:

- We are God's helpers. We should try to help when we see that an animal is not being taken care of or bullied.
- God's children also never ignore stray animals. We should help them find a safe place to stay.
- God's children know that animals have feelings too. That's why we should treat them well. If they are lonely or look sad, we should comfort them with cuddles. If they are unhappy, we should try to find out why. Go give your pet a hug right now!

Something to Think About:

God takes good care of me. So I should do my best to protect and take care of the animals He created.

Super Saying:

What does "by perseverance the snail reached the ark" mean?
Answer: Never give up; keep on trying to reach your goal even if it takes long.

What Are You Doing, Mr. Ant?

> Take a lesson from the ants, you lazybones. Learn from their ways and become wise! Though they have no prince or governor or ruler to make them work, they labor hard all summer, gathering food for the winter.
>
> Proverbs 6:6-8

Who would have thought that King Solomon would watch the little ants in his palace so closely!

The ants in King Solomon's fine palace were exactly the same as today's ants. They also ate plants and scraps of food.

As soon as the grains, veggies or fruit are ripe, hardworking ants all over the world get to work. They march to their nests in one long row. Each one carries a piece of food much bigger than their tiny bodies.

When the long winter arrives, their storerooms are filled with delicious food. Then it is their time to rest.

Today, ants eat all kinds of food that King Solomon's ants did not know about at all. Just like we do, ants today eat fries, chocolates and even burger scraps. Junk food is just as unhealthy for them as it is for us!

Even though ants are much smaller than we are, we can still learn a few lessons from them:

1. Ants are hardworking.
2. They do not need a leader to tell them what to do.
3. They don't need to be kept in line all the time.
4. Ants always start on time.
5. They do not stop until they have finished their task.

Don't you think these are good enough reasons to not use ant poison to kill them? Rather sprinkle talcum powder to keep them away.

More about Ants:

- There are different colors of ants: red, black, yellow and brown.
- Ants live together in a nest.
- Their nests are almost like gigantic cities made from mud.
- There can be more than 5 million ants living in one nest.
- The most important ant in the nest is the queen. She is not really the leader; she is an egg-producing machine. It is her job to lay thousands of eggs a day!
- Each ant in the nest has a specific task.
- Together they keep the nest safe and sound.
- Ants can carry more than their weight.

The Shepherd and His Sheep

God will feed His flock
like a shepherd. He will
carry the lambs in His arms,
holding them close to His heart.
Isaiah 40:11

The more sheep a person owned in Bible times, the richer they were. That's why a sheep owner hired a shepherd to look after the sheep. The shepherd had to make sure the sheep had fresh water and enough grass to eat every day. He also had to keep the wolves and bears away from the sheep.

The shepherd knew every single sheep. He knew them so well that he could tell which sheep was afraid of thunder and which one liked to scurry off after butterflies. At the end of each day, the shepherd counted his sheep, and kept them safely in a pen.

These days we are not allowed to keep sheep in a city or in a town. How rich we are is also not measured by the number of sheep we own. Today we use a bank card or a piggy bank.

It is still loads of fun to visit a farm. You can watch how the sheep are sheared or help feed the little lambs with a bottle.

God cares for us just like a shepherd. If we are tired, He carries us in His arms. If we are sad, He holds us close to His heart. He is our heavenly Father.

All we have to do is to be obedient little lambs. We must listen to His voice and follow in His footsteps. If we get lost, God will come and look for us until He finds us, just like a shepherd would look for a lost little lamb.

More about Sheep:

- A female sheep is called an ewe.
- A male sheep is called a ram.
- Sheep can live for up to 10 years.
- A sheep's woolly coat can keep him warm and cool him down.
- Sheep can hear very well.
- Sheep can remember people and other sheep's faces for a few years.
- A lamb can recognize his mother's voice among many other sheep.
- A sick sheep knows which bushes to eat from to make him feel better.

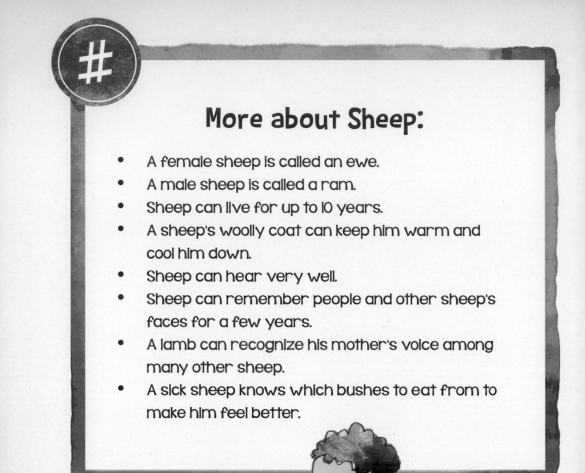

Something to Think About:

Little lambs are gentle and
they do not fight with each other.
Let's also try to be like little lambs.

Super Saying:

What does it mean to do something
"in two shakes of a lamb's tail"?
Answer: To do something very quickly.

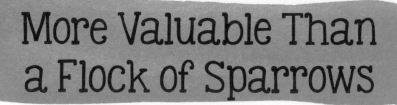

More Valuable Than a Flock of Sparrows

"What is the price of five sparrows – two copper coins? Yet God does not forget a single one of them. So don't be afraid; you are more valuable to God than a whole flock of sparrows." Luke 12:6-7

Sparrows are such cheerful birds. You can hear a flock of sparrows approaching from far away. They chatter and chirp just like friends who have lots of stories to tell each other.

Sparrows like to make their nests near people, because they know there is always food and pieces of cloth and wool to build a cozy nest. They also know when there are children in the house who might throw breadcrumbs out on the grass so they have something to eat. Or if there is a bird feeder in the garden where they can feast all day long – almost like their own 5-star hotel!

Jesus knows sparrows very well. In Bible times, He probably watched them play in the grain fields and look for crumbs in the marketplace. Perhaps their chirping and singing also made Him smile.

In Bible times, sparrows weren't worth much. You could buy five sparrows for just two cents! That is why Jesus told a story about sparrows in Luke 12. He said, "Sparrows are not worth a lot of money but God still loves them. He cares for them every day by giving them a warm place to sleep and enough food to eat. He never forgets a single one of them. Do you know that God cares for you much more than for sparrows? You are precious to Him from your head to your toes. That's why you do not need to worry about anything. God will care for you even better than He cares for the sparrows."

More about Sparrows:

- Mr. Sparrow builds the nest.
- Mrs. Sparrow lays three to five eggs.
- They can have chicks three times a year.
- Baby sparrows are rather hasty: within only a few weeks of hatching, they leave the nest.
- Sparrows do not walk, they hop.
- Sparrows can live for 4-5 years.
- A sparrow can fly approximately 38 kilometers per hour.

Something to Think About:

God knows every single sparrow and will never forget any one of them. You are worth more to Him than many sparrows!

Super Saying:

What does it mean to be "an early bird"?
Answer: To get up really
early in the morning.

The Elegant Mr. Raven

Elijah did as the Lᴏʀᴅ told him and camped beside Kerith Brook, east of the Jordan. The ravens brought him bread and meat each morning and evening, and he drank from the brook.
1 Kings 17:5-6

The raven looks very elegant in his shiny, black suit. You can hear them from quite far away when they call "caw-caw-caw" – like someone who wants to say something very important!

Ravens feel at home in the big city. They visit parking lots and nibble on breadcrumbs on the school playground. They are just as comfortable living on a farm. But they give the farmers a lot of trouble because they want to peck at all the shiny things.

In Bible times, there were also ravens. Noah sent a raven out of the ark to look for dry ground.

But the most beautiful story about ravens is found in 1 Kings 17. It is the story of how God sent Elijah to Kerith Brook to hide there. He promised Elijah that the ravens would bring him food.

Elijah obeyed God. He went to hide away just like God had asked him to do. He was all alone, far away from people and there were no shops. He drank water from the brook and the ravens brought him meat and bread every morning and every evening.

God kept His promise. He and the ravens were Elijah's best friends.

More about Ravens:

- Ravens have very strong beaks and legs.
- Their feathers shine in the sunlight.
- Ravens eat insects, mice, frogs, rabbits and small birds.
- You can teach a raven to speak.
- They are excellent imitators and can mimic a telephone, car, a blender and even a dog.
- Ravens have an excellent memory and can actually count!
- Can you believe it? A healthy raven will help a sick one.

Something to Think About:

God sent ravens to give Elijah food.
God always takes care of us,
just like He took care of Elijah.

Super Saying:

What does it mean when
you say, "In fine feather"?
Answer: It means that a person is in
a good mood and finds things funny.

Gooing Doves of Peace

After His baptism, as Jesus came up out of the water, the heavens were opened and He saw the Spirit of God descending like a dove and settling on Him. And a voice from heaven said, "This is My dearly loved Son, who brings Me great joy."
Matthew 3:16–17

It is so much fun to go for a walk in the park. Soon a whole flock of doves might gather at our feet. They flutter around and coo. It sounds like they are saying, "Give us some crrrumbs! Give us some crrrumbs!"

Mom once showed me a dove with a sore leg. I decided to feed that one first. She hopped closer and pecked the popcorn pip from my hand. She turned her head to the side and looked at me. I think she knew she had made my heart glad.

The Bible also tells us about doves. A dove brought an olive branch back to Noah in the ark. That was how Noah knew the earth was starting to dry up after the flood!

David wished he had wings like a dove (see Psalm 55:6). He felt tired and wanted to fly far away to a quiet place where no one would bother him for a while.

Jesus saw a very special dove. After John baptized Him in the Jordan River, it looked as if the heavens opened up. A dove came down and went straight to Jesus. It was God's Holy Spirit. God was very happy with Jesus. God said, "Jesus is My dear Son. He is very close to My heart!"

Even today a dove still reminds millions of people across the world of peace, love and the Holy Spirit.

More about Doves:

- When a male and female dove get together, they stay together for the rest of their lives.
- When a dove pecks seeds off the ground, he doesn't swallow straightaway, he keeps the seed in his crop.
- Only the males "coo-coo".
- The females lay at most two eggs in a nest.
- Both Mr. and Mrs. Dove feed the baby doves. The first few days the baby doves only get crop milk. It's not real milk, but just as nutritious.
- A dove can find its way back, even if it is hundreds of kilometers away from home.
- In the old days, doves were used to deliver important messages. They were called carrier pigeons.

Something to Think About:

I can be a messenger of love and peace, just like a dove!

Super Saying:

What does it mean to be
"as harmless as a dove"?
Answer: To be a peaceful person.

Hello, Mr. Locust

It was the worst locust plague in Egyptian history, and there has never been another one like it. They devoured every plant in the fields and all the fruit on the trees. Not a single leaf was left on the trees and plants. Exodus 10:14-15

A big fat locust jumped on my chest yesterday! I got such a fright! Dad said, "Don't be afraid. He just likes the bright red color of your jersey!" Then Dad removed him from my jersey, and we looked at him closely. Locusts have very strong legs that help them to jump high and far. There are little thorns on their legs to protect them – almost like gladiators!

While we were inspecting the locust, he moved his antennae (feelers). I think he was a little shy.

John the Baptist was not scared of locusts. He lived in the desert where there wasn't a lot of food and quickly learned that locusts were a tasty snack.

Locusts also taught the Pharaoh of Egypt a good lesson. Pharaoh let God's people work like slaves. God wanted to punish Pharaoh and set His people free. So God told Moses to stretch out his staff over Egypt. Suddenly a strong easterly wind started blowing. The wind brought big swarms of locusts. The Egyptians had never seen so many locusts before. Everywhere they looked, the locusts were gnaw-gnaw-gnawing at some-thing. Not a single green leaf was left. The evil Pharaoh was pale with fright! He knew then that God was so powerful that He could even control nature!

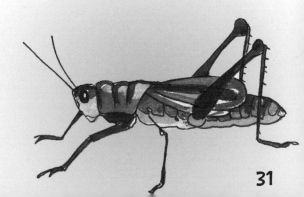

More about Locusts:

- A locust has six legs and four wings.
- They have pincers to help them tear off leaves.
- Their ears are on their bellies!
- Some locusts rub their hind legs against each other or against their wings. This makes a strange noise!
- Mrs. Locust is bigger than Mr. Locust.
- A locust can jump one meter.
- Just like John the Baptist, people in Africa and South America today also eat locusts as snacks.
- One locust cannot cause a lot of damage, but a swarm of locusts can ruin a farmer's entire harvest.
- Locusts sometimes spit brown fluid to protect themselves from enemies.

Something to Think About:

God will do anything to help His children ...
He'll even send a swarm of locusts
to teach evil people, like Pharaoh,
a lesson.

Super Saying:

What does it mean to be
"knee-high to a grasshopper"?
Answer: It means to be
very young or very small.

A Big Catch of Fish

He said, "Throw out your net on the right-hand side of the boat, and you'll get some!" So they did, and they couldn't haul in the net because there were so many fish in it. There were 153 large fish.
John 21:6, 11

When Granddad goes fishing, he always brings some fish back for us. When I pick up the big shiny fish it feels as slippery as soap. I am going to draw a picture of it in my school exercise book. I know my teacher will give me a gold star! It will glimmer just as brightly as the fish's shiny scales!

Granny usually cleans the fish and fries it in a pan. Sometimes she makes fries with the fish. Granddad says fish is good for your brain.

Some of Jesus' disciples were fishermen. They liked to make a fire and fry fish. Sometimes they managed to catch a whole bunch of fish at once. At other times they struggled to catch anything. One time, after a long night of trying to catch fish, the disciples felt discouraged. They hadn't caught a single fish for breakfast. Jesus watched them from the shore. "Throw your nets out on the other side of the boat," Jesus said. The disciples did what Jesus told them to do. It wasn't long before their nets were filled with fish.

When they reached the shore, a small fire was already burning with fish and bread ready to eat. Though their mouths were watering, the disciples counted the fish that they had caught. There were 153 large fish!

"Come have some breakfast," Jesus invited them. Then He handed out the fish and bread.

Everyone ate. They were happy and content.

More about Fish:

- Fish make good pets.
- They breathe through their gills.
- A fish's body is covered with scales and slime. This helps them move easily through the water.
- Some fish can look like the bottom of the ocean. This is to camouflage themselves and hide from their enemies.
- Most fish species cannot distinguish between colors.
- Flying fish don't really fly, they just glide over the water.
- A seahorse is also a fish - although it doesn't look like one!

Something to Think About:

Because the disciples listened to Jesus, they caught a lot of fish. We must always do what God tells us to do

Super Saying:

What does it mean to be "like a fish in water"? Answer: To feel happy and comfortable doing something.

The Humble Donkey

Mary was engaged to Joseph and traveled with him to Bethlehem. She was soon going to have a baby.

Luke 2:5 CEV

In Bible times, the people did not have cars. Everyone had to walk where they needed to go. Some people were fortunate enough to have a donkey. The poor donkey had to work very hard.

Today, people don't really know how valuable a donkey can be. They only see their dull coat and two long ears. But they don't know that donkeys are really clever, loyal and gentle animals. They also don't know that a donkey is a friend that will stand by you through thick and thin. They will even chase away people who want to hurt you!

Mary, Jesus' mother, rode on the back of a donkey to Bethlehem just before Jesus was born.

Balaam's donkey stopped in the middle of the road when he saw an angel. When Balaam got mad at the donkey, the donkey started to speak. Balaam got the fright of his life!

Jesus was a true friend to the donkeys. Of all the animals on earth, He chose to ride on the back of a donkey into the city of Jerusalem for the Passover feast. The people heard that Jesus was on His way. They put palm leaves on the ground together with their coats. It looked like a carpet! Others waved the palm branches like flags. They joyfully shouted, "Praise God in the highest heaven!"

It was a special day, not only for Jesus and the people, but also for the donkey.

More about Donkeys:

- A young male donkey is called a colt.
- A female donkey is called a jenny.
- Their baby is called a foal.
- The sound that donkeys make is called "braying".
- They are very clever and have excellent memories.
- Donkeys' big ears help to keep them cool.
- A herd of donkeys always pick the strongest one as their leader.
- Donkeys don't like the rain or getting wet. It makes them sick.
- Donkeys are excellent at looking after sheep.

Something to Think About:

Jesus is a friend of the donkey. That's why I should always treat a donkey with respect.

Super Saying:

What does it mean to "talk the hind legs off a donkey"? Answer: It means to talk a lot.

Before the Rooster Crows ...

Peter said, "Lord, I am ready to go to prison with You, and even to die with You." But Jesus said, "Peter, let Me tell you something. Before the rooster crows tomorrow morning, you will deny three times that you even know Me."
Luke 22:33-34

Mr. Rooster lifts his head from under his wing very early in the morning. He shakes his feathers and shouts: "Cock-a-doodle-doo!"

Now everyone on the farm knows it is time to get out of bed.

Jesus spoke to His disciples about a rooster. It was one dark night. He knew the soldiers were on their way to arrest Him. Peter didn't want Jesus to leave them. He said, "I will follow wherever You go. Even if I have to go to prison with You. Or I'll even die with You!"

Jesus answered, "Before the rooster crows tomorrow morning, you will deny three times that you even know Me." Later that night soldiers came to arrest Jesus. Peter followed them. He wanted to see what was happening. A lady recognized Peter and asked, "Wasn't that man with Jesus?"

Peter got a big fright. "I don't know Jesus," he lied. Two more people recognized Peter as Jesus' friend, and he told them as well, "I don't know Jesus!"

Before Peter had even finished answering the third time, the rooster crowed. Suddenly he remembered what Jesus had told him. Then he went outside and cried bitterly.

More about Roosters:

- A rooster has a red comb on its head that looks like a fancy crown. It also has an extra claw on the back of each leg called a spur. It is used for fighting.
- Years ago, a rooster was one of the only alarm clocks available. He would crow in the morning and wake everyone up. A young rooster starts crowing at four months old.
- A rooster protects the hens and chicks in the yard.
- Sometimes a rooster also clucks to indicate to the other chickens where they can find food.
- Roosters perform a little dance called tidbitting. They move their heads up and down, dragging their wings on the ground. Do you think you can do it?

? **Something to Think About:**

I do not want to be scared to say that I know Jesus. Next time I see a rooster, I will remember to be brave and stand up for Jesus.

" **Super Saying:**

What does "don't count your chickens before they hatch" mean?
Answer: Do not plan on something happening before it actually happens.

Soar on Wings Like Eagles

Those who trust in the LORD
will find new strength. They
will soar high on wings like eagles.
Isaiah 40:31

As we were hiking through the fields, Dad said, "Look there! High up in the sky!" He pointed to a tiny black speck in the sky.

It was moving closer and closer. "It's an eagle, the king of the birds," said Dad. Eagles have giant wings. They can fly really high. When they are high up in the sky, they soar for hours on the air currents. Almost like giant kites. They make their nests high up on cliffs or rock ledges, where they lay their eggs and look after their chicks.

While an eagle soars in the sky, it spots and keeps its eye on its prey until it swoops down and catches it. Then the eagle takes it to the nest and the eaglets eat to their hearts' delight.

The Bible speaks about eagles a few times. God says when we are discouraged, we must trust in Him. He will give us new strength, so that we will be able to soar high on wings like eagles. He will make us so strong that we will never get too tired again!

God also promises that He will take good care of us. Just like an eagle teaching its chicks to fly. The mother eagle is always ready to swoop down and catch the little ones when they get tired. She catches them on her wings and carries them safely back to the nest.

More about Eagles:

- Eagles are symbols of strength and freedom.
- They often appear on emblems or flags.
- An eagle's beak looks like a big hook.
- Eagles mostly eat meat and catch reptiles, birds, fish, and other small animals.
- Eagles are much like people; some have neat and clean nests, and others' nests are untidy.
- The typical wingspan of an eagle is 2.5 meters.
- An eagle can see more colors than a human can.
- American Indians used to give eagle feathers to each other as gifts.

Something to Think About:

I should never give up. God will give me new strength to fly high on eagles' wings!

Super Saying:

What does it mean to "watch someone with an eagle's eye?" Answer: To watch them very closely and carefully.

The Merry Ostrich

"An ostrich proudly flaps her wings. Once she starts running, she laughs at a rider on the fastest horse."
Job 39:13, 18 CEV

In our broom closet, we have a pink feather duster made from ostrich feathers. I like that duster very much.

"You're playing with the feather duster more than we use it to dust the house," Mom says, teasing me.

She knows my friends and I use it in our make-believe circus and concerts. Our favorite part is to dance around and pretend to be little ostriches. We flap our wings and tiptoe in a circle. When we are tired of all the dancing, Mom pours freshly squeezed fruit juice for all of us. "Come, take a break, all you merry ostriches!" she says.

Last year Dad took us to an ostrich farm. There we learnt everything about ostriches. We could touch the ostriches and watch how they ran in a race. I stood on a real ostrich egg. The shell is so hard that it didn't even crack!

In the Bible, God and Job talked about all kinds of important things ... even about ostriches! Job said Mrs. Ostrich flaps her wings when she is happy. She lays her eggs on warm soil so they can hatch easily. She handles them quite roughly and is not even scared that they will break.

God did not make ostriches to be very clever but He made them to be very special. They are so special that they can outrun a horse without much effort!

More about Ostriches:

- They are the biggest of the bird species in the world.
- Ostriches cannot fly and only have two toes on each foot.
- Ostriches do not need to drink water. Their bodies make their own water.
- An ostrich's eye is bigger than its brain.
- Ostriches use their wings as umbrellas to keep their chicks cool.
- The male ostrich likes to show off and strut in front of the female. He opens his wings like a giant fan.
- One ostrich egg is as big as 24 chicken eggs.
- They live for 50 to 75 years.

Something to Think About:

Just like the ostrich, God also
made me in a very special way.
I want to be His merry little ostrich.

"

Super Saying:

What does it mean to "bury your head
in the sand" like ostriches do?
Answer: To ignore a problem
and hope it goes away.

The King Lion

Daniel answered, "Long live the king! My God sent His angel to shut the lions' mouths so that they would not hurt me, for I have been found innocent in His sight. And I have not wronged you, Your Majesty."
Daniel 6:21–22

The lion is the king of the animal world. His paws leave huge footprints in the sand. His mane flutters like a royal robe in the wind. When he roars, the whole forest becomes quiet. All the animals listen carefully – from the tiniest mouse to the tallest giraffe, they all listen to what the lion has to say.

People are also very afraid of lions. If you come across a lion in the wild, and there is no tree nearby to hide in, you are in big trouble!

We read about lions in the Bible too. A young lion once attacked Samson. The Spirit of God came over Samson. Suddenly he became very strong. He killed the lion with his bare hands.

Daniel was brave too. He did not want to worship any other gods besides God. As punishment, he was thrown into a den of lions. Daniel didn't care. He knew God was stronger than all the lions in the whole world. When the king came to the lions' den the following morning, Daniel did not have a scratch on him. God made sure the lions' mouths stayed shut.

Even the lion listens when the King of the Universe speaks!

More about Lions:

- Lions like to be around their family.
- A family of lions is called a pride.
- Lions talk to each other by roaring.
- It is the male lion's job to protect his family and their territory.
- It's the female lion's job to hunt for food. They are very clever, and hunt in groups.
- The male eats first and afterwards the female and cubs eat.
- Lions can run 80 kilometers per hour.
- Lions are real sleepy heads. They sleep up to 16 hours per day!

Something to Think About:

Even King Lion listens when God speaks. That's why I should do my best to listen and obey God too.

Super Saying:

What does it mean to be "lionhearted"?
Answer: To be very courageous and brave.

Glip-Glop Goes the Horse

"Have you given the horse its strength or clothed its neck with a flowing mane? Did you give it the ability to leap like a locust? Its majestic snorting is terrifying! It paws the earth and rejoices in its strength."
Job 39:19-21

There are many horses on Uncle Charlie's farm. Each one has its own stable with his or her name on the stable door, like Duke, Melody and Buttercup.

At first, I was a little scared because the horses are so big. But I soon realized that I have no reason to be afraid.

Early in the mornings I walk with Uncle Charlie to the stables. The horses can hear us coming, and peek out of their stable doors. Melody makes soft neighing sounds. She cannot wait for me to pat her head.

If I help Uncle Charlie in the stables, I can ride on Melody's back. It makes both our hearts glad. When the two of us gallop through the fields, it feels like we are flying!

The Bible tells us how special horses are. They are very strong, with beautiful manes and can jump very high. Kings and princes always rode on majestic horses – each one with its own special saddle and bridle. Horses were not used to work like their donkey cousins. Sometimes they had to deliver urgent messages. Other times they fought in battles. The sound of their hooves on the ground made the enemy tremble with fear.

Pharaoh chased after the Israelites with fast horse-drawn chariots when they left Egypt.

God sent a horse-drawn chariot of fire that took Elijah to heaven. Wow, I wish I could have seen that!

More about Horses:

- A male horse is called a stallion.
- A female horse is called a mare.
- A baby horse is called a foal.
- The sound that horses make is called "neighing".
- A pony is a special small type of horse.
- Horses mostly eat hay, which is a type of grass.
- They can sleep while standing!
- A foal can start to walk and run just after it is born.
- A horse's height is measured in hands. A pony for example is 14 hands high.
- You look at a horse's teeth to find out how old it is.

Something to Think About:

God made horses to be proud animals. I should also be proud because I am God's child.

Super Saying:

What does it mean when you tell someone to "hold your horses"? Answer: You are asking the person to slow down and be patient.

As Strong as an Ox

He owned 7,000 sheep, 3,000 camels, 500 teams of oxen, and 500 female donkeys. He also had many servants. He was, in fact, the richest person in that entire area.

Job 1:3

An ox is big and strong with huge horns. Before there were trains and trucks, oxen were used to transport heavy loads. Twelve oxen were usually harnessed in front of a wagon. Grain or vegetables were loaded on the wagon. The person leading the oxen walked in the front. He had to choose the best route through the fields.

The wagon driver sat in the coach box. He held the reins. He also had a long whip that he hit with a "cracking" sound on the ground. The oxen knew this sound. It meant that they had to move onward!

A good wagon driver never hit his oxen. He knew each one by name, and looked after them very well. After a long day, the oxen were unharnessed and could graze in the fields. That was their time to rest!

The Bible also speaks about oxen. Job was a very rich man. He had 7,000 sheep, 3,000 camels, 500 female donkeys and 500 teams of oxen. Just imagine how many wagons Job's oxen could pull! Job used his oxen to plow his land.

Just like we have today, there were rules to make sure people took good care of their animals. One of the rules was that no one was allowed to keep an ox from nibbling on grain while they were busy working (see 1 Corinthians 9:9).

More about Oxen:

- In some countries, instead of using trucks, oxen are still used to transport goods.
- Oxen eat grass, herbs, moss, green plants, and wheat.
- An ox is born a bull.
- When a yoke is put on an ox's shoulders, he can pull a heavy load.
- An ox can pull heavier loads than a horse, and can endure hard work for much longer.
- In some countries oxen wear horseshoes.
- Oxen have split hooves, so each hoof needs two horseshoes.

Something to Think About:

In biblical times rules already existed to protect animals. I should also protect animals!

Super Saying:

What does it mean to be as "strong as an ox"?
Answer: To be very strong.

A Camel through the Eye of a Needle

"It is easier for a camel to go through the eye of a needle than for a rich person to enter the Kingdom of God!"
Matthew 19:24

I would really like to ride a camel one day. Just like the wise men in the Bible who followed the star to Bethlehem to see Baby Jesus. I will sit high up on the camel's back rocking back and forth. Then I will say, "Good job, Mr. Camel."

The Bible is filled with stories about camels. Jacob sent 30 camels to his brother Esau who was mad at him. By doing that he was saying, "I'm sorry."

The queen of Sheba traveled with a large caravan of camels to see for herself how rich King Solomon was. The camels were loaded with spices, lots of gold and precious jewels.

John the Baptist's clothes were made from camel hair. Kings and princes didn't want to wear clothes made from camel hair, because it was too scratchy. But John did not mind. It kept him cool in summer, and dry and warm in winter.

Jesus also talked to His disciples about a camel. He said that a rich man easily forgets that everything he owns belongs to God. Because they own so many nice things, it is harder for them to give everything they own away and to follow Jesus. That is why Jesus said that "it's easier for a camel to go through the eye of a needle, than it is for a rich man to give away his possessions and follow Me."

More about Camels:

- A camel is sometimes called the ship of the desert.
- They are clever and can hear and see very well.
- There are two types of camels: the dromedary or one-humped camel, and the Bactrian with two humps.
- Calves are born without humps. There is no water in a camel's hump, only fat.
- Camels eat grass, seeds, branches and plants with thorns.
- They have two sets of lashes to keep the sand and dust out of their eyes.
- A camel can close its nostrils to keep the sand out.
- A camel spits to protect itself.

Something to Think About:

A camel reminds me that everything I have belongs to Jesus. That's why I share what I have with others.

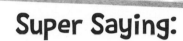

Super Saying:

What does it mean when someone says that it would be easier to get "a camel through the eye of a needle"?
Answer: The situation seems impossible.

The Seven Fat Cows

I saw seven fat, healthy cows
come up out of the river. But then I saw
seven sick-looking cows, scrawny and
thin, come up after them. These thin,
scrawny cows ate the seven fat cows.
Genesis 41:18-20

Mom buys milk in a bottle. I drink a big glass of milk every morning. "Now you have a white moustache!" Mom laughs and gives me a hug.

Our black cat also wants some milk. I fill his bowl, and he drinks it all. "Now Kitty has a white moustache too!" I laugh and give him a hug. Uncle Ken and Aunt Milly don't buy milk. They have a cow that produces milk for them to drink. Uncle Ken gets up early in the morning to milk Daisy. He wants to milk Daisy himself, because she is very special!

The Bible also speaks about cows. While Joseph was unfairly put in prison in Egypt, Pharaoh dreamt that seven fat cows walked out of the river and grazed in the grass. Then seven thin cows came out the water. The seven thin cows ate the seven fat cows!

Pharaoh wanted to know what his dream meant. Joseph was the only person who could help him. He said, "Your majesty, for the next seven years there will be plenty of food throughout the land of Egypt. But afterward there will be seven years of famine. You should gather all the food produced in the good years and store it away. That way there will be enough to eat when the seven years of famine come to the land of Egypt."

"Wow, you are so clever!" said Pharaoh.

"It is God who shows me what the dreams mean," said Joseph.

More about Cows:

- The moo sound that a cow makes is called lowing or bellowing.
- A cow's milk is kept in her udder.
- There are teats on the udder. When you squeeze the teats, the milk comes out.
- If you treat a cow well, she will produce lots of milk.
- Cows like to sleep close to their families, just like humans!
- They also have best friends, usually two to four.
- In the old days, each family had its own cow to milk.
- A cow drinks about a bathtub full of water a day.

Something to Think About:

Pharaoh's dream was all about saving while they could. Next time I get sweets or pocket money, I should try to save some too.

Super Saying:

What does it mean to do something "until the cows come home"?
Answer: To do it for a very long time.

Feeding the Pigs

"He persuaded a local farmer to hire him, and the man sent him into his fields to feed the pigs. The young man became so hungry that even the pods he was feeding the pigs looked good to him. But no one gave him anything."

Luke 15:15-16

I like to sit on Granddad's lap. He takes my hand, unfolds my fingers one by one, and says:

"This little piggy went to market,
This little piggy stayed home.
This little piggy had roast beef
This little piggy had none.
And this little piggy went
Wee, wee, wee, all the way home!"

When Granddad reaches the "wee" part, he tickles me until I am all out of breath. Then Granny says, "Calm down you two. I'm going to make us a pot of tea now."

As soon as Granny opens the cookie jar, Granddad and I are the most well behaved little pigs you have ever seen!

The Bible also speaks about pigs. A son asked his father for all the money he would inherit from him one day, and traveled to a far-off land. He made many new friends and had one party after the other. Then his money ran out. All of a sudden, he had no money and no place to stay.

His so-called friends were all gone. The only job he could find was to feed pigs. The young man was so hungry that he ate the pods that he was supposed to feed to the pigs.

One day the son thought, "My father's servants have more food to eat than I have now. I will return home tomorrow and ask to be one of his servants." Shortly afterwards he returned home. His dad was overjoyed to see him. He arranged a big feast. His lost son had come home. He did not have to feed pigs ever again.

More about Pigs:

- A female pig is called a sow.
- A male pig is called a boar.
- Pigs are cleverer than we think.
- You can teach them to do tricks and perform certain tasks.
- Pigs love company.
- Certain types of pigs can make great pets.
- Pigs eat more or less the same food as humans.
- A pig's nose is called a snout.
- Pigs' hair is used to make paint brushes.

Something to Think About:

Even though I sometimes behave badly, like the son in the Bible story, God is glad when I turn back to Him!

Super Saying:

What does it mean to "eat like a pig"?
Answer: To eat a lot or to make
a lot of noise while you eat.

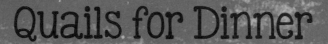

Quails for Dinner

The LORD said to Moses, "I have heard the Israelites' complaints. Now tell them, 'In the evening you will have meat to eat, and in the morning you will have all the bread you want.'" That evening vast numbers of quail flew in and covered the camp.
Exodus 16:11–13

I like to visit our neighbor, Uncle Peter. In his backyard, he has huge birdcages. In one of the cages are parakeets. In another one are canaries. And yet another is filled with doves. They twitter and sing and coo for all they're worth.

I like to look for feathers on the ground and stick them in my sun hat. At first, I did not even notice the shy quails walking around on the ground. Their grey and brown color make them look just like the bushes.

Uncle Peter says quails are biblical birds because God sent them as food to the hungry Israelites in the desert.

During Bible times, the Israelites were traveling through the desert for a long time. They were tired, dusty and hungry. Everybody complained to Moses. Then God made a special plan. In the mornings, He sent them sweet bread called manna. The Israelites picked it up off the ground and ate as much as they wanted.

At nighttime God sent quails. A whole flock would come flying down and land between their tents. It was easy for the Israelites to catch them and cook them. Everyone was happy. Finally, they had enough to eat. Nobody went to bed hungry. Moses was also happy. The Israelites could now see for themselves that God provided for them, just as He had promised.

Today quail meat and eggs are very expensive. They are only sold in special shops. I think Moses would smile at this!

More about Quails:

- Quails like to be alone.
- During autumn, they flock together.
- Some types of quails have crests (or plumes) on their heads that bounce up and down when they walk.
- They can only fly short distances.
- They eat seeds, insects and grain.
- Quails build their nests on the ground with grass.
- A female quail can lay between 10 and 20 eggs at a time.
- Sometimes the females look after each other's young.
- Enemies of quails are cats, skunks, foxes, snakes, owls, dogs and humans.

Something to Think About:

God promised that He would take care of the Israelites - and He did. That's why He will keep His promises to me as well.

Super Saying:

What does it mean to "quail" at
something or someone?
Answer: To be afraid of something or someone.

Stop the Little Foxes!

Catch all the foxes, those little foxes, before they ruin the vineyard of love, for the grapevines are blossoming!
Song of Solomon 2:15

I was so frightened when I heard a fox howl for the first time. We had gone camping. We quickly put up our tent and then Dad, my brother and I looked for pieces of wood to make a fire. My mom and sister prepared our camp beds.

At sunset, everything was set up around the campsite. Before long, we sat around the campfire roasting marshmallows. Dad was telling us one story after the other. Then suddenly we heard "ahooooo!"

My sister's eyes were as big as saucers. She jumped on Dad's lap. When we heard "ahoooo" again, I also wanted to jump and hide my head under Dad's jacket.

"Don't be afraid," Dad said. "It's only a fox calling his friend. They will not come any closer. They are too scared of fire." The next day we found small fox paw prints in the sand. Now I know that I don't have to be afraid of them.

The Bible also tells us about foxes. King Solomon knew how the small foxes liked to nibble on the grapes. That's why he warned that the little rascals should be caught early – while the vineyards were still blossoming. We must also be on the lookout every day, like King Solomon, for the small things that want to ruin our day – just like the little foxes!

More about Foxes:

- Foxes are from the dog family.
- They usually walk alone.
- Foxes eat meat.
- They hunt during the night.
- Foxes can hear very well – even when something moves underground, they can hear it.
- They are good at climbing trees.
- Foxes have whiskers to help them navigate and find their way.
- Baby foxes are born blind without any hair on their skin.

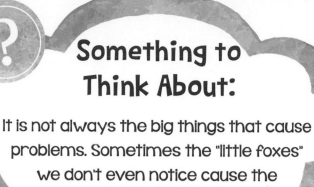

Something to Think About:

It is not always the big things that cause problems. Sometimes the "little foxes" we don't even notice cause the most trouble.

Super Saying:

What does it mean to be "as sly as a fox"?
Answer: To be crafty
or tricky, even cunning.

The Partridge Is Tricked

Like a partridge that hatches eggs she has not laid, so are those who get their wealth by unjust means. At midlife they will lose their riches; in the end, they will become poor old fools.
Jeremiah 17:11

Granddad puts on his hat and takes his walking stick. His dog knows when it is time to go for a walk. He runs to the basket at the front door and takes out his leash. Then he sits and waits patiently for Granddad to put it on him. Before long the two are on their way.

I like to walk with them, especially early in the mornings, or late afternoons. That is when the partridges make their cackling sounds. Sometimes there are babies with them. They run so fast that I can barely see their thin legs move.

Every time I hope to find a partridge's nest. I want to see what their eggs look like. Granddad says it is not likely that we will find them. The mother partridges are far too clever for that. They hide their eggs very well.

The prophet Jeremiah spoke about a partridge that hatched eggs she did not lay. She thought she had a whole nest full of eggs, when only a few belonged to her. When the eggs hatched, everyone would have been able to see that only a few of the chicks belonged to her.

People who get rich by cheating are just like the partridge. One day everyone will know about their cheating!

More about Partridges:

- Partridges enjoy company and like to socialize in groups. They are family of the pheasant.
- They can fly, but prefer to walk around on the ground.
- Partridges eat seeds, but the chicks also eat insects.
- Partridges make their nests on the ground.
- The chicks already start running around shortly after they've hatched.
- Both the male and female look after the chicks.
- Their enemies are foxes, dogs, birds of prey and people.

Something to Think About:

It is never right to steal or want what others have. Learn to be content with what you have.

Super Saying:

What does it mean to say, "don't put all your eggs in one basket"? Answer: Don't concentrate all your efforts on only one thing.

Hyraxes in the Crevice

High in the mountains live
the wild goats, and the rocks
form a refuge for the hyraxes.
Psalm 104:18

Hyraxes are cute fluffy animals with shiny eyes and black snouts. They almost look like rabbits but without long ears. Because they do not have claws to dig holes in the ground, they live in rock crevices.

As soon as the sun rises in the mornings, they creep out of their crevices and look for a sunny spot. The bigger ones sleep in the sun while the little ones play around. In some parks or picnic places, the hyraxes are very tame and are not afraid of people. They even come closer to look for food.

Although I want to feed them, I know that it is not allowed. Our food is not good for them and feeding them makes them lazy. Then they no longer want to look for food, because they learn to beg when we feed them. I will rather take a good photo. That is so much better for the hyrax and for me!

The book of Psalms is jam-packed with songs that King David wrote for God. He said God is great and strong and so wonderful! His heart rejoiced at how God cares for the blue skies, the clouds and the ocean. He makes springs bubble with water and He makes the birds sing. He makes the high mountains with special rock crevices for hyraxes to hide away.

Hyraxes might be small, but God made them strong enough to run playfully up very steep cliffs – something that people can't do!

More about Hyraxes:

- Hyraxes have thick fur and eat only plants.
- They move in groups of 10 to 80.
- They spend most of the day sitting in the sun.
- They have special "watchmen" that look out for any danger.
- When it rains, they don't leave their hiding places.
- Hyraxes have flat nails like elephants. Only the inside toe on each foot has one long nail that they can scratch themselves with.
- Hyraxes make 21 different sounds while talking to each other.

Something to Think About:

Even though I sometimes feel as small as a hyrax, God made me strong and clever enough to do many wonderful things.

Super Saying:

What does it mean to have your "day in the sun"?
Answer: To suddenly get a lot of attention.

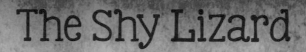

The Shy Lizard

On this earth four things are small but very wise: Ants ... badgers ... locusts ... lizards, which can be caught in your hand, but sneak into palaces.
Proverbs 30:24-28 CEV

On the front porch among Mom's pots and plants, lives a tiny lizard. He has huge eyes and feet that look like little hands. On each foot there are tiny fingers.

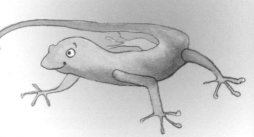

He is very shy and hides most of the time. Sometimes, when he thinks that no one is watching, he comes out of his hiding place. Then he sits in the sun or catches insects.

I sit and watch him. Can you believe it? He knows how to run upside down on the porch ceiling!

I want to know how he does it. I also want to run upside down on the ceiling!

The Bible tells us about lizards too. King Solomon made a list of four animals in the book of Proverbs that can do clever things. The lizard is on his list. Here is what King Solomon said:

1. Ants are not strong, but they know how to store food in summer for the winter.
2. Hyraxes look like they are weak, but they know how to make their homes among the rocks.
3. Locusts have no king, but they can march like an army.
4. Lizards can easily be caught with bare hands. But they sneak into kings' palaces, where no one else dares go.

The shy lizard is a real rascal!

More about Lizards:

- Lizards, iguanas and chameleons are family.
- The smallest lizard is only about 2 cm long.
- Lizards have special toes that help them climb.
- They do not have eyelids, so they lick their eyes to keep them moist.
- They "chat" with each other by making chirping sounds.
- Some lizards drop their tails when they are threatened by danger. Their tails mostly grow back.
- Sometimes a lizard returns to the place where he lost his tail ... and if he finds it, he eats it!

Something to Think About:

Even though a lizard is shy, he can still do astonishing things. If you are shy, you can still be good at a lot of things.

Super Saying:

What does it mean to be "like a chameleon"? Answer: You can change your attitude and behavior to fit any situation.

Where Are You Off to, Mrs. Stork?

"Even the stork that flies across the sky knows the time of her migration, as do the turtledove, the swallow, and the crane. They all return at the proper time each year. But not My people! They do not know the LORD's laws."

Jeremiah 8:7

Mrs. Stork looks very smart with her black and white feather coat, sharp beak and long, red legs. She is never in a hurry. She walks with long strides through the wetlands looking for something to eat.

Sometimes it looks like she is on the way to deliver a very important message. That must be the reason why artists like to paint pictures of storks on greeting cards!

In some countries, storks build huge nests in trees, on church towers, roofs or even telephone poles. High up there, Mrs. Stork's chicks are safe.

During autumn, storks fly thousands of kilometers to warmer regions. They never lose their way. When the seasons change, and it is spring again, they return home – to the exact same place, city, town, and the exact nest. Without the use of a map or GPS!

The Bible also tells us about storks. The prophet Jeremiah was upset because the Israelites were disobedient. He wished they would be more like storks.

Storks, just like turtledoves, swallows and cranes, know the proper time to return home. But the Israelites did not know when to stop turning away from God. Jeremiah wished they were more like the stork and her family who know when and how to return straight home – straight home to God who was waiting for them with open arms.

More about Storks:

- Storks are graceful when they fly – almost like ballerinas.
- They can live for 20 to 30 years.
- Storks live together in groups.
- Most of them like to build their nests near wetlands and swamps.
- They do not really deliver babies as some people believe.
- Storks use their long bills to catch fish, frogs and other small animals.
- Storks cannot sing the way most birds can. They can hiss or clatter their bills together.
- Some storks are like garbage removers because they eat dead animals and in so doing keep the area clean.

Something to Think About:

I want to be like a stork.
I want to fly straight home -
straight into God's arms.

Super Saying:

What does it mean to
"get a visit from the stork"?
Answer: It means that a mommy and
daddy are going to have a baby soon.

Beware of the Wolf!

"Beware of false prophets who come disguised as harmless sheep but are really vicious wolves. You can identify them by the way they act."
Matthew 7:15-16

Wolves are special animals. They are clever, brave and true to their pack. They do not like to live close to people. They want to hunt for food undisturbed.

Unfortunately, the forests where they and many other animals live are being cut down. As the woods shrink, there is less and less food for them to eat. That is why they start hunting farm animals.

A pack of hungry wolves can wreak havoc. Almost as bad as the wolf who ate the granny in Little Red Riding Hood. Or the wolf who blew down the houses of the three little pigs!

When farmers are upset because the wolves hurt their animals, they just want to get rid of the culprit. Fortunately, there are animal lovers who work to make sure wolves are protected.

The Bible also tells us about wolves. These wolves come disguised as sheep. They are false prophets trying to steal people away from God. They may seem as meek as lambs but they are in fact hungry wolves out to cause trouble.

Jesus said that we would know when we encounter one of these wolves. We must just watch carefully what they do and say and we will quickly see that a child of God does not act that way.

More about Wolves:

- Wolves are an endangered species - this means that they are protected and people aren't allowed to hurt them.
- They like company and live together in groups.
- Each pack has a leader. They defend their territory against other wolves. Their only enemy is people.
- Wolves have big feet.
- They can smell 100 times better than people.
- A female wolf has four to six pups per year.
- Wolves hunt at night and sleep during the day. They only eat meat and are rather greedy because they swallow their food without really chewing.
- Wolves are members of the dog family.

Something to Think About:

Look out for people who pretend to be good, but are really evil. They don't act like children of God.

Super Saying:

What does it mean to be "a wolf in sheep's clothing"?
Answer: To be a dangerous person pretending to be harmless.

Covered in Spots

Can a leopard change his spots?
In the same way, Jerusalem, you
cannot change and do good, because
you are accustomed to doing evil.
Jeremiah 13:23 NCV

Mom made me a tracksuit. It is brown with black spots, just like a real leopard's spots.

When I wear my tracksuit, Mom draws whiskers on my face. Dad gives me one of his ties to use as a tail.

I growl and run through the house. I climb in the tree and peek through the leaves. I once waited for my sister to walk past under the tree. I wanted to scare her with a loud "Grrrrrrr!" I waited and waited and waited … and I became sleepier and sleepier.

The next moment I fell to the ground with a "thud!" Mom and Dad came running out of the house. When they saw that I was fine, we all had a good laugh.

My sister came running around the corner of the house. She was also laughing. "A leopard fell out of our tree!" she giggled and pulled my tail.

The Bible also tells us about leopards. The prophet Jeremiah was angry at the Israelites. He told them about the leopard's spots. He said that the Israelites were so used to doing wrong things that their bad habits stuck to them like the spots of a leopard. Just like they will never break their bad habits, the spots will also not disappear, no matter what they do.

More about Leopards:

- Leopards are fast and can jump long distances.
- They like to be alone.
- Each leopard has its own territory.
- Leopards hunt at night. During the day they rest in trees or caves.
- Their spots camouflage them to make it harder to spot them in trees.
- Black leopards also have spots; they are just difficult to see.
- Leopards purr when they are happy, just like a kitty cat!

I don't want to start bad habits that stick to me like a leopard's spots.

Super Saying:

What does "a leopard can't change its spots" mean?
Answer: Even if you pretend to be something else, you cannot change who you are.

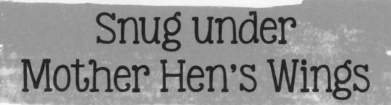

Snug under Mother Hen's Wings

"How often I have wanted
to gather your children
together as a hen protects
her chicks beneath her wings."
Matthew 23:37

After laying her eggs, our white hen Penny sat down on her nest. I cannot wait for the eggs to hatch!

"How many eggs do you think there are, Mom?" I ask. "That is Penny's secret," says Mom. "You'll have to ask her." I walk to the chicken coop. Penny's nest is right at the back in the corner. "How many eggs do you have, Penny?" I ask nicely.

All that Penny says is "cluck-cluck". Then she puts her head under her wing and falls asleep.

"Penny doesn't want to share her secret with me," I told Mom later. "We will find out soon enough," says Mom and winks. A few days later, we heard "peep! peep! peep!" Then a whole lot of golden chicks peeped out from under Penny's feathers.

Penny got up almost like she wanted to say, "The secret is out! Aren't they beautiful!"

Then she gathered the chicks and kept them safe beneath her wings. The best place on earth!

The Bible also tells us about a hen. God is like a mother hen to us and we are His chicks. He loves us very much. That's why He looks after us so well. He keeps us safe under His wings – every night and every day. From the time we were little babies until we grow old, He will care for us. He will never let us wander too far from His safe wings.

More about Hens:

- Hens are gentle and care very well for their chicks.
- They are popular pets.
- The oldest hen ever recorded was 16 years old.
- If you meddle with a hen's chicks, she gets really upset.
- A hen can lay up to 300 eggs a year.
- She turns each egg about 50 times a day – that is hard work.
- A hen feels safe when her rooster is close by.
- A hen can recognize almost 100 people.
- A hen cannot taste sweet things.

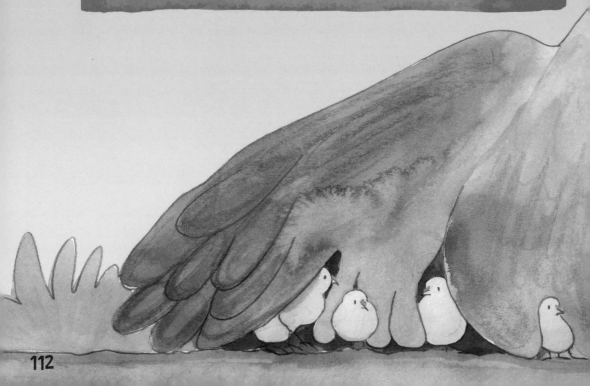

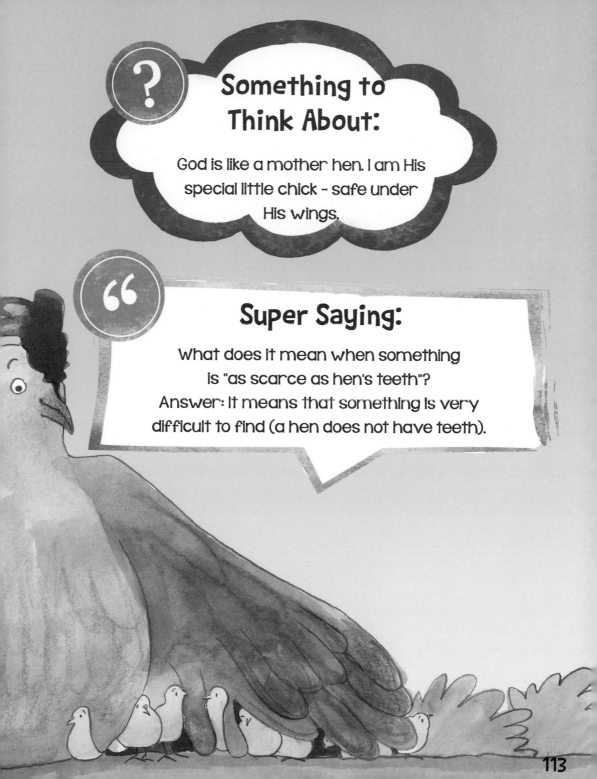

Something to Think About:

God is like a mother hen. I am His special little chick - safe under His wings.

Super Saying:

What does it mean when something is "as scarce as hen's teeth"?
Answer: It means that something is very difficult to find (a hen does not have teeth).

All the Goats to the Left!

All the nations will be gathered
in His presence, and He will separate
the people as a shepherd separates
the sheep from the goats.
He will place the sheep at His
right hand and the goats at His left.
Matthew 25:32-33

In springtime, the fields are green and lush. The birds wake us with a different tune every morning. The sheep have little white lambs and the goats have little white kids. Some skip around in the field, and others sleep close to their mothers.

At the end of the day, the shepherd whistles loudly. The shepherd's dog barks joyfully. He helps to gather the sheep and goats together. From the biggest ram to the smallest little lamb, they all come running. The shepherd whistles again. It means: "All the sheep to the right!" In a jiffy the dog gathers the sheep to the right side of the shepherd.

When the shepherd whistles for a third time, it means: "All the goats to the left". The dog runs and gathers all the goats to the left side of the shepherd. "There we go!" says the shepherd pleased. "Tomorrow is another day!"

The Bible also tells us about sheep and goats. In the book of Matthew, Jesus says that God is our Shepherd and we are the sheep and goats. He will one day come to gather us together. He will separate the ones who believe in Him and are good. They will stand on the right to go with Him to heaven. Those who were bad and didn't listen to God are like goats. They will stand on God's left side, and stay behind. Oh dear!

More about Goats:

- A male is called a billy.
- A female is called a nanny.
- A baby goat is called a kid.
- The sound that a goat makes is called bleating.
- Not only the rams have horns, some ewes also have horns.
- Goats are very nosey. Anything out of the ordinary catches their attention.
- A goat knows its name and comes when it is called.
- Goats are very agile. Some can walk around high up in the mountains, and others can even climb trees.
- Did you know that goats have no upper front teeth?

Something to Think About:

Make sure that you are like
a good sheep who obeys
God, not like a naughty goat.

Super Saying:

What does it mean to separate
the sheep from the goats?
Answer: To separate the good from the bad.

The Spider's Web

The same happens to all who forget God. The hopes of the godless evaporate. Their confidence hangs by a thread. They are leaning on a spider's web.
Job 8:13-14

When I walked to our mailbox this morning, I saw a brand-new spider's web in the daisy bush. The spider neatly spun it between four bright yellow daisies. The threads were so fine that I could barely see them. On every corner dewdrops glistened like bright lights. The web rocked slowly back and forth in the breeze.

"Good morning, Mrs. Spider!" I said. "You must be so tired! Did it take a long time to spin your new home? Where is the living room? Show me your kitchen?"

The spider just sat quietly in the middle of her web. She did not move a single leg! She waited for a juicy fly to get caught in her web … just in time for breakfast!

In biblical times Job also saw how hard the spider worked to spin a web. Maybe he also liked the shiny threads in a spider's web rocking gently in the breeze.

Job said someone who has forgotten God, has nothing to lean on. When times are tough and they get into trouble, they have nothing to hold on to. Instead of having a strong rope, they only have the threads of a spider's web to hold on to. And they break in an instant.

You think you are still leaning on something strong, but then it has fallen over. You grab hold of something, but the thread snaps!

More about Spiders:

- Spiders have eight legs.
- They are family of scorpions.
- Spiders spin their webs with silky threads.
- Only a few types of spiders are poisonous to people.
- Spiders have claws on each leg, which keep them from being stuck in their own web.
- A spider's blood is blue.
- House spiders can run up a wall because of the hair under their feet.
- The trapdoor spider lives in a tunnel with a little door.
- Sometimes a male spider gives a fly to the female as a gift!

God's New Earth

In that day the wolf and the
lamb will live together; the leopard will
lie down with the baby goat. The calf
and the yearling will be safe with the lion,
and a little child will lead them all.

Isaiah 11:6

We are all familiar with wild animals. A wolf looks for a juicy lamb to eat. The leopard scouts for the first deer to devour for breakfast. And the lion looks for the fattest calf.

In nature, the weakest animals become the food of the stronger ones. That's why animals always need to run or hide. It is only in storybooks that they are best friends.

But in the book of Isaiah, we find an important promise from God. He said that the weakest animals would one day live in peace with the strong ones on His new earth. There everything will be different.

The wolf and goat will be best friends. The leopard will fall asleep between the lambs. No animal will be afraid of another.

The cow and bear will eat together. The bear cub and the calf will play together. The lion will not feel like eating other animals. He will even taste a piece of grass every now and then!

The baby will play safely near the hole of a cobra. A little child will put its hand in a nest of deadly snakes without harm.

In God's new earth, there will be no sadness. As the waters fill the sea, so the earth will be filled with good things from God.

Something to Think About:

God has a special plan for animals in His new earth. He has a special plan for you, too!

Super Saying:

What does it mean to be "as meek as a lamb"?
Answer: To be shy, quiet and gentle.